Collins Primary Maths
Pupil Book 2

Series Editor: Peter Clarke

Authors: Andrew Edmondson, Elizabeth Jurgensen,
Jeanette Mumford, Sandra Roberts

Contents

Topic	Objective	Pages
Place value, ordering and rounding (whole numbers)/Measures	To multiply or divide any integer up to 10 000 by 10 (whole-number answers), and understand the effect To use symbols correctly, including less than (<), greater than (>), equals (=) To round any positive integer less than 1000 to the nearest 10 or 100 To recognise negative numbers in context (e.g. on a number line, on a temperature scale)	5, 6, 7
Mental calculation strategies (+ and −)/Understanding addition and subtraction	To add 3 or 4 small numbers, finding pairs totalling 10, 9 or 11 To add three two-digit multiples of 10 To add/subtract a pair of two-digit numbers (crossing the 10 but not the 100 boundary) To partition into tens and units, adding the tens first	8, 9, 10
Pencil and paper procedures (+ and −)/Rapid recall of addition and subtraction facts	To develop and refine written methods for column addition/subtraction of two whole numbers less than 1000: adding the least significant digits first/decomposition To develop and refine written methods for money calculations To know by heart all number pairs that total 100 To derive quickly all pairs of multiples of 50 with a total of 1000	11, 12, 13, 14, 15, 16
Problems involving "real life" and money/Making decisions	Use addition and subtraction to solve word problems involving numbers in "real life" or money, using one or more steps	17
Measures: (mass)/ Making decisions	To know the equivalent of one half, one quarter, three quarters and one tenth of 1 kg in grams To measure and compare using kilograms and grams To choose and use appropriate number operations and appropriate ways of calculating (mental, mental with jottings, pencil and paper) to solve problems To record measurements using mixed units, or the nearest whole/half/quarter unit (e.g. 3·25 kg)	18, 19, 20
Measures: (mass)/Problems involving measures (mass)	To use all four operations to solve word problems involving numbers in measures (mass), using one or more steps	21
Shape and space: (position and direction/angle and rotation)/2D/3D/Reasoning about numbers and shapes	To recognise simple examples of horizontal and vertical lines To visualise 3D shapes from 2D drawings and identify simple nets of solid shapes To use the eight compass directions N, S, E, W, NE, NW, SE, SW To start to draw, measure and order a set of angles less than 180° To make shapes: for example, construct polygons by paper folding or using pinboard, and discuss properties such as lines of symmetry To solve mathematical problems or puzzles, recognise and explain patterns and relationships, generalise and predict. Suggest extensions by asking "What if…?"	22, 23, 24, 25, 26, 27, 28, 29, 31, 32, 33, 34
Measures: (time)	To estimate/check times using seconds, minutes, hours	30

Properties of numbers and number sequences	To recognise and extend number sequences formed by counting from any number in steps of constant size, extending beyond zero when counting back	35, 36
Reasoning about numbers	To solve mathematical problems or puzzles, recognise and explain patterns and relationships, generalise and predict To make and investigate a general statement about familiar numbers by finding examples that satisfy it	37, 38, 39
Understanding multiplication and division/Rapid recall of multiplication and division facts/Checking results of calculations	To know by heart multiplication facts for 2, 3, 4, 5 and 10 times tables To derive quickly doubles of multiples of 10 to 500, and the corresponding halves To begin to know multiplication facts for the 6 times table To begin to know multiplication facts for the 8 times table	40, 41, 42, 43
Understanding multiplication and division/Mental calculation strategies (× and ÷)/Problems involving "real life" money/Checking results of calculations	To use × and ÷ to solve word problems involving numbers in "real life" and money, using one or more steps: explain and record methods To use closely related facts (e.g. to multiply by 9, multiply by 10 and adjust)/(e.g. to multiply by 11, multiply by 10 and adjust)	44, 45, 46, 49
Mental calculation strategies (×)/Pencil and paper procedures (×)	To partition (e.g. 23 × 4 = (20 × 4) + (3 × 4)) To develop and refine written methods for TU × U – partitioning	47, 48
Fractions and decimals	To identify two simple fractions with a total 1 To recognise the equivalence of simple fractions To order simple fractions: for example, decide whether fractions such as $\frac{3}{8}$ or $\frac{7}{10}$ are greater or less than one half To understand decimal notation and place value for tenths and hundredths, and use it in context	50, 51, 52, 53, 54
Organising and interpreting data	To solve a problem by collecting quickly, organising, representing and interpreting data in tables, charts, graphs and diagrams, including those generated by a computer, for example: bar charts – intervals labelled in 2s/5s/10s/20s	55, 56, 57, 58, 59, 60, 61, 62, 63

Acknowledgements

The publisher would like to thank the following for their valuable comments and advice when trialling and reviewing Collins Primary Maths 4 materials.

Concetta Cino – Barrow Hill Junior School, London
Mrs B Crank – Heron Hill County Primary, Kendal, Cumbria
Elizabeth Fairhead – Puttenham C of E School, Guildford, Surrey
Mrs D Kelley – Green Lane First School, Bradford
Alison Lowe – Goddard Park Primary School, Swindon
Sarah Nower – Watchetts Junior School, Camberley, Surrey
Miss M Richards – Birchfield Primary School, Birmingham
Mrs S Simco – Heron Hill County Primary, Kendal, Cumbria
Janice Turk – Sacred Heart Junior School, London
Chris Wilson – Woodville School, Leatherhead, Surrey

• Multiply or divide any integer up to 10 000 by 10 (whole-number answers), and understand the effect   Sp 1, 1

Blast off tens

Refresher

1 Multiply each number by 10.

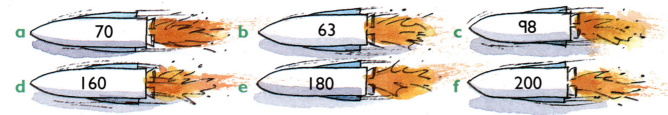

a 70   b 63   c 98
d 160 e 180 f 200

2 Divide each number by 10.

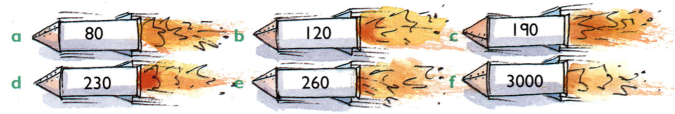

a 80   b 120 c 190
d 230 e 260 f 3000

Practice

1 Multiply each number by 10.

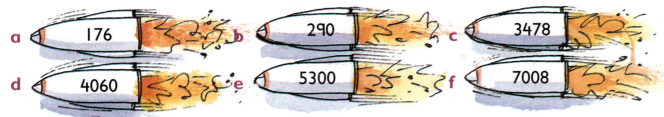

a 176   b 290   c 3478
d 4060 e 5300 f 7008

2 Divide each number by 10.

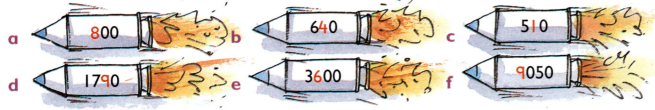

a 800   b 640   c 510
d 1790 e 3600 f 9050

3 Write the value of the red digits in question 2.
4 A full bag contains 10 flying saucer sweets.
  How many bags can be filled?

a 90   b 350   c 2900    d 7040

5

- Use symbols correctly, including less than (<), greater than (>), equals (=)

Sp 1, 2

Crocodile comparisons

2 < 5   9 > 4   6 = 6
less than greater than equals

Refresher

1 Copy the following and write <, > or = between the numbers.

a 20 ☐ 90   b 70 ☐ 30   c 59 ☐ 72
d 71 ☐ 17   e 89 ☐ 98   f 23 ☐ 23
g 100 ☐ 90   h 77 ☐ 66   i 19 ☐ 99

Practice

1 Copy the following and write <, > or = between the numbers.

a 294 ☐ 492   b 864 ☐ 846   c 469 ☐ 1284
d 4523 ☐ 2951   e 8516 ☐ 8592   f 3652 ☐ 3649
g 5000 ☐ 5010   h 632 ☐ 623   i 2004 ☐ 2040

2 Copy and fill in the missing numbers on the number line.

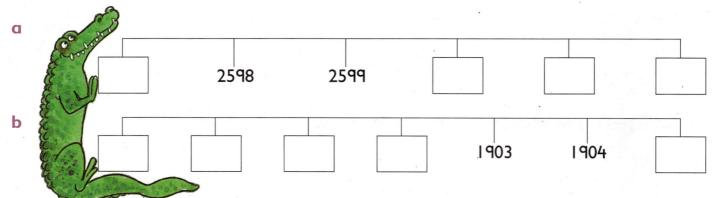

a ☐ 2598 2599 ☐ ☐ ☐

b ☐ ☐ ☐ ☐ 1903 1904 ☐

3 Copy these weights. Write your own weights in the spaces. They must be in order.

a 395g _____ 412g   b 2908g _____ 3064g   c 6000g _____ 6030g

d 6294g _____ _____ 7000g   e 1090g _____ _____ _____ 1109g

- Round any positive integer less than 1000 to the nearest 10
- Record estimates and readings from scales to a suitable degree of accuracy
- Recognise negative numbers in context

Sp 1, 3

Outdoors measuring

Refresher

1 Round the weights to the nearest 10 g.

a 51 g   b 65 g c 32 g d 14 g e 96 g

2 Estimate the weights of the pine cones.

Practice

1 Round the weights to the nearest 10 g.

a 135 g   b 2192 g c 1845 g  d 3098 g e 2006 g

2 Estimate the weights of the logs.

3 Read the thermometers and write down the temperatures.

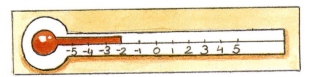 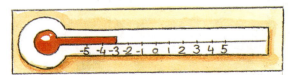

4 Copy and complete the number line.

−6   6

Finding pairs

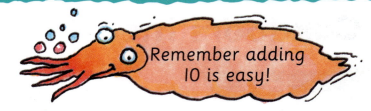

Remember adding 10 is easy!

Refresher

1. Work out the calculations finding pairs of numbers that equal 9, 10 or 11.

   Write out the calculation in the order you add it up.

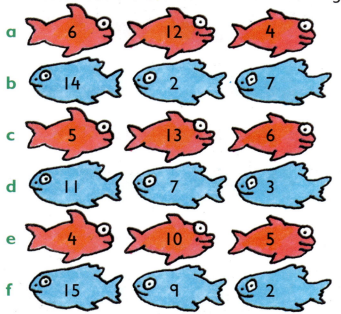
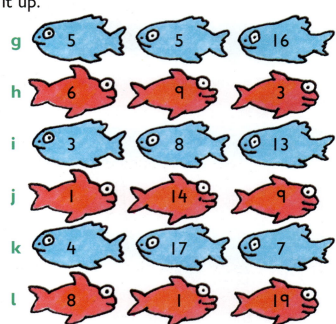

Practice

1. Work out the calculations finding pairs of numbers that equal 9, 10 or 11.

   Write out the calculation in the order you add it up.

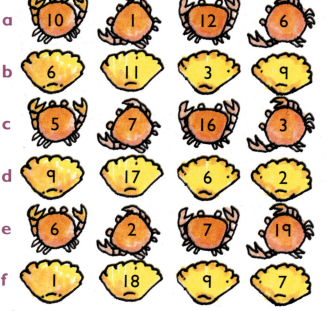
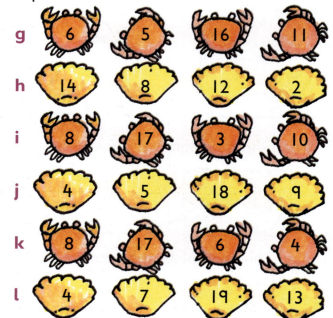

• Add three two-digit multiples of ten

Sp 2, 2

Cake addition

Refresher

1. Look at the cakes. Make up 5 calculations adding two of the numbers together.

2. Make up 10 calculations adding three of the numbers together.

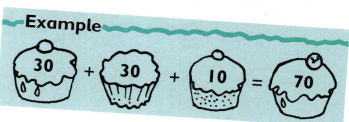

Practice

1. Look at the cakes. Make up 20 calculations adding three of the numbers together.

9

- Add/subtract a pair of two-digit numbers (crossing the 10 but not 100 boundary)
- Partition into tens and units adding the tens first

Sp 2, 3

Turn of the cards

Look at the pairs of cards that have been turned over and use the two numbers to make an addition and subtraction calculation.

Refresher

Example
26 + 42 = 68
20 + 6 + 40 + 2 = 68

a) 22, 46   b) 64, 32   c) 76, 21

d) 55, 32   e) 53, 27   f) 25, 48

g) 76, 18   h) 64, 29   i) 56, 31

Practice

Example
42 − 26
42 − 20 − 6 = 16

a) 68, 29   b) 57, 28   c) 17, 76

d) 39, 56   e) 63, 28   f) 74, 18

g) 43, 27   h) 55, 36   i) 64, 27

- Develop and refine written methods for column addition of two whole numbers less than 1000

Sp 2, 4

Column addition

Refresher

Work out the calculations vertically. Write the answer on one line. Then choose five calculations and write out the tens and units you have added.

Example

```
 46
 32 +
 78
```

```
 46
 32 +
  8  units
 70  tens
 78
```

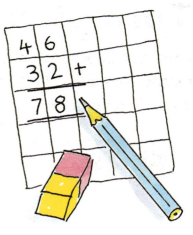

a 43
   26 +

b 74
   23 +

c 61
   37 +

d 22
   76 +

e 53
   24 +

f 17
   81 +

g 62
   35 +

h 45
   42 +

i 73
   21 +

j 28
   71 +

Practice

Work out the calculations vertically. Write the answer on one line. Then choose five calculations and write out the hundreds, tens and units you have added.

Example

```
 156
  43 +
 199
```

```
 156
  43 +
   9  units
  90  tens
 100  hundreds
 199
```

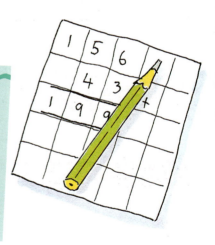

a 106
    53 +

b 273
    24 +

c 316
    82 +

d 350
    37 +

e 461
    38 +

f 543
    52 +

g 625
    71 +

h 737
    62 +

i 614
    75 +

j 508
    81 +

11

- Develop and refine written methods for column addition of two whole numbers less than 1000

Sp 2, 5

Carrying numbers

Refresher

Work out these calculations vertically. You will need to carry the units into the tens column.

Example
```
 345
  37 +
 ───
 382
   1
```

a 265 + 28
b 215 + 47
c 426 + 68
d 206 + 79
e 517 + 44
f 448 + 34
g 327 + 58
h 559 + 37
i 718 + 75
j 608 + 48

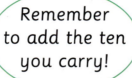

Remember to add the ten you carry!

Practice

Work out these calculations vertically. You will need to carry either the tens or the units.

Example
```
 734
  92 +
 ───
 826
   1
```

a 254 + 39
b 368 + 25
c 417 + 67
d 523 + 59
e 605 + 88
f 734 + 92
g 683 + 46
h 775 + 74
i 788 + 51
j 591 + 75

Column subtraction

Copy each calculation out and work it out vertically.

Example
```
 84
 52 −
 ―――
 32
```

Refresher

a 84 − 52   b 68 − 32

c 75 − 21   d 98 − 45

e 79 − 55   f 64 − 42

g 58 − 16   h 74 − 51

i 83 − 32   j 93 − 72

4 − 2 is 2 and 80 − 50 is 30 so the answer is 32.

Practice

a 576 − 53   b 494 − 62

c 563 − 21   d 692 − 70

e 867 − 26   f 969 − 25

g 857 − 13   h 795 − 72

i 884 − 61   j 948 − 20

Column calculations

Refresher

1 Copy out the calculations and work them out vertically.

a 493 − 62
b 675 − 54
c 784 − 34
d 892 − 61
e 579 − 47

Example
```
 465
  33 −
 432
```

2 These calculations need the units digit changing.

a 276 − 48
b 352 − 18
c 664 − 27
d 574 − 36
e 895 − 57

Example
```
 2 7⁶1̸6
   4 8 −
 2 2 8
```

Practice

1 Copy out the calculations and work them out vertically. These calculations need the units digit changing.

a 655 − 38
b 796 − 49
c 851 − 25
d 972 − 38
e 670 − 42

Example
```
 6 ²3̸₁4
   1 7 −
 6 1 7
```

2 These calculations need the tens digit changing.

a 738 − 63
b 847 − 73
c 653 − 81
d 742 − 61
e 575 − 92

Example
```
 ⁶7̸ ₁2 7
   5 7 −
 6 7 0
```

- Develop and refine written methods for money calculations

Sp 3, 3

Bookseller calculations

Refresher

Example
£4·71
£3·36 +
£8·07

1 The bookseller needs to find out the price of each box of books. Add the price of the books in each box.

a £3·62 / £2·27

b £1·46 / £2·31

c £4·50 / £3·37   d £2·14 / £3·43   e £4·34 / £1·35

2 The bookseller sells one of the books in each box. Work out the price of the book that is left.

a £5·47 / £2·34 −
d £6·64 / £3·11 −

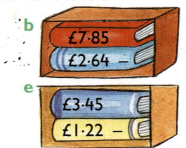
b £7·85 / £2·64 −
e £3·45 / £1·22 −

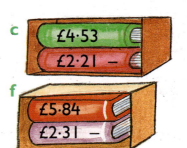
c £4·53 / £2·21 −
f £5·84 / £2·31 −

Practice

1 The bookseller needs to find out the price of each box of books. Add the price of the books in each box.

a £2·68 / £3·15
d £2·82 / £4·51

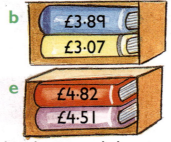
b £3·89 / £3·07
e £4·82 / £4·51

c £4·35 / £3·26
f £3·12 / £2·96

2 The bookseller sells one of the books in each box. Work out the price of the book that is left.

a £6·37 / £2·09 −
d £5·24 / £1·63 −

b £7·64 / £4·17 −
e £9·38 / £6·52 −

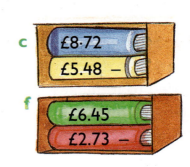
c £8·72 / £5·48 −
f £6·45 / £2·73 −

- Know by heart all number pairs that total 100
- Derive quickly all pairs of multiples of 50 with a total of 1000

Sp 3, 4

Find the pair

Refresher

Look at the red numbers on the hundred square. Find the number that, when added to it, makes 100. Use the hundred square to help you. Write the pair of numbers as an addition calculation.

Example
14 + 86 = 100

1	2	3	4	5	6	7	8	9	10
11	12	13	14	15	16	17	18	19	20
21	22	23	24	25	26	27	28	29	30
31	32	33	34	35	36	37	38	39	40
41	42	43	44	45	46	47	48	49	50
51	52	53	54	55	56	57	58	59	60
61	62	63	64	65	66	67	68	69	70
71	72	73	74	75	76	77	78	79	80
81	82	83	84	85	86	87	88	89	90
91	92	93	94	95	96	97	98	99	100

Practice

1. Choose a number from the bag. Work out the number that, when added to it, makes 100. Write the pair of numbers as an addition calculation. Write 10 calculations.

Example
26 + 74 = 100

2. Choose a number from the bag. Work out the number that, when added to it, makes 1000. Write the pair of numbers as an addition calculation. Write 10 calculations.

Example
50 + 950 = 1000

- Use addition and subtraction to solve word problems involving numbers in "real life" or money

Sp 3, 5

Which method?

Work out the problems. Decide which method you are going to use. You may change the method you use depending on the calculations involved.

What is the calculation I need to do?

Refresher

a Louise timed how long she spent doing her homework one week. On Monday it took her 35 minutes and on Wednesday it took 16 minutes. How long did it take altogether?

b Jack has £2·12 and Liz has 77p. How much do they have altogether?

c The bookshop ordered 250 copies of a new monster book. Eighty-seven of them sell on the first day. How many are left?

d I have 46p. How much more do I need to make £1?

e Dan has 100 stickers. Sixty-eight are in his album and the rest are hidden in his bedroom. How many are in his bedroom?

f A bee keeper has 165 pots of honey. He sells 71 pots of honey in a day. How many does he have left?

Practice

Remember: show all your working

a I counted how many cars went past my window. On Saturday, 178 went past and on Sunday, 89. The total for Saturday, Sunday and Monday was 353. How many went past on Monday?

b I want to buy a book that costs £5·50. I get 85p pocket money a week. I have been saving for three weeks. How much more money do I need?

c There are 286 children in the assembly sitting on the floor and there are 87 sitting on chairs. 56 of the children leave the hall. How many are left?

d The teachers have 230 biscuits in the staff room over a term. Mrs Stevens eats 41 of them. Mr Lee eats 56. Mrs Goods will not say how many she has eaten but there are 81 biscuits left. How many did she eat?

e I have £10. I spend £2·67 on my lunch and £3·50 to get into the cinema. How much do I have left?

17

- Know the equivalent of one half, one quarter, three quarters and one tenth of 1 kg in grams

Sp 4, 1

Weighing – up or down

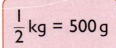

Use the scales to help you

$\frac{1}{2}$ kg = 500 g

Refresher

1 Write these weights in grams.

  a $\frac{1}{2}$ kg   b 1 kg   c $\frac{1}{4}$ kg

  d $\frac{3}{4}$ kg   e $\frac{1}{10}$ kg

2 Find sets of things that weigh about 100 g. Make a list.

Example

12 marbles weigh about 100 g

Practice

1 Write these weights in grams.

  a 3 kg 250 g   b 5 kg 100 g

  c 9 kg 500 g   d 3 kg 400 g   e 4 kg 900 g

Example
3 kg 125 g = 3000 g + 125 g = 3125 g

2 Write these weights in kilograms.

  a 6500 g   b 7100 g

  c 5250 g   d 8750 g

Example
3500 g = 3000 g + 500 g = $3\frac{1}{2}$ kg

3 You have these standard weights.

100 g

200 g

500 g

a  TEA 400 g

b  CRUNCH! 700 g

c 1300 g

d  1600 g

Check the weights of these packets.
Use the least number of weights each time.

4 Round the weights of these parcels to the nearest 100 g.

a  570 g

b  935 g

c  1860 g

d  2345 g

- Measure and compare using kilograms and grams
- Choose and use appropriate number operations and appropriate ways of calculating ... to solve problems

Sp 4, 2

Balancing to 50 g

Refresher

1 This is Rita's recipe for raspberry crumble.

450 g raspberries   250 g flour   150 g sugar   100 g butter

She has these weights.   Write the weights she uses to measure:

a flour   200 g + ____ g

b raspberries

c sugar

d butter

Practice

1 You have a supply of these weights:

a Find 3 ways to balance 350 g using the 50 g, 100 g and 200 g weights.

b Find 6 ways to balance 750 g using the 4 standard weights.

Example

350 g = 100 g + 100 g + 100 g + 50 g

2 Find ways of measuring out amounts of rice using only two standard weights. Make drawings to show how you worked it out.

Example

150 g = 100 g + 50 g

150 g + 50 g = 200 g

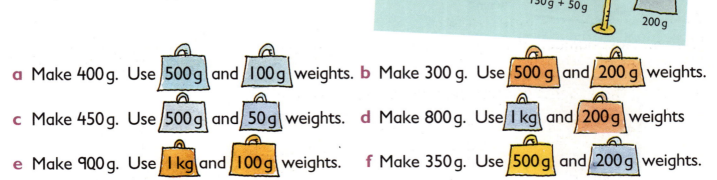

a Make 400 g. Use 500 g and 100 g weights. b Make 300 g. Use 500 g and 200 g weights.

c Make 450 g. Use 500 g and 50 g weights. d Make 800 g. Use 1 kg and 200 g weights

e Make 900 g. Use 1 kg and 100 g weights. f Make 350 g. Use 500 g and 200 g weights.

- Record measurements using mixed units, or the nearest whole/half/quarter unit (e.g. 3·25 kg)

Sp 4, 3

Cookhouse problems

Refresher

1 Work out what each lunch weighs.
  a   b   c

Weights of food
hamburger 125g | apple 150g
sandwiches 150g | orange 250g
baked potato 250g | banana 175g
quiche 75g | drink 250g
crisps 25g

2 Write which lunch is: a just over $\frac{1}{2}$ kg?   b $\frac{3}{4}$ kg?   c about $\frac{1}{4}$ kg?

Practice

1 Copy and complete this table.

Weight of 1 item	Number of servings			Total weight of 10	
	2	4	10	kg and g	kg
hamburger 125 g	250 g	500 g	1250 g	1 kg 250 g	1·25 kg
quiche 75 g					
baked potato 250 g					
sandwiches 150 g					
banana 175 g					

2

How many 30 g servings in this packet of cereal?

3

Each pot of yoghurt weighs 120 g. Find in kilograms the weight of a tray of 12 pots.

4

This box holds 30 packets of crisps. What is the weight of crisps in:

a 1 box?   b $\frac{1}{2}$ box?   c 3 boxes?

- Use all four operations to solve word problems involving numbers in measures (mass), using one or more steps | Sp 4, 4

Weights work-out

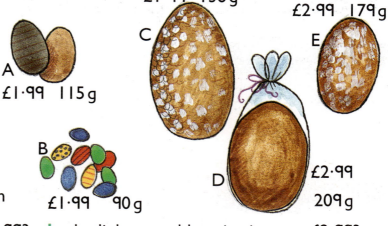

Refresher

1 Look at these eggs.
  Write which egg is the best buy

  a at £2·99   b at £1·99

2 What is the difference in weight between

  a the lighter and the heavier item at £1·99?   b the lighter and heavier item at £2·99?

Practice

900 g

600 g

1 kg 250 g

500 g

1 kg

400 g

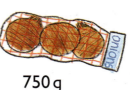

750 g

1 What is the approximate weight in grams of:

  a 1 potato   b 1 chicken thigh   c 1 pepper   d 1 onion   e 1 tub of yoghurt?

2 a How much heavier is the chicken than the packet of spaghetti?
  b How much lighter are the peppers than the onions?

3 The quiche is for 5 people. Roughly how many grams are in one portion?

4 How much spaghetti is left after 4 people each have a 90 g serving?

5 Work out in kilograms, the total weight of food in each wire basket.

21

• Recognise simple examples of horizontal and vertical lines

Horizontal and vertical lines

Refresher

1 For each object decide whether the purple line is horizontal or vertical.

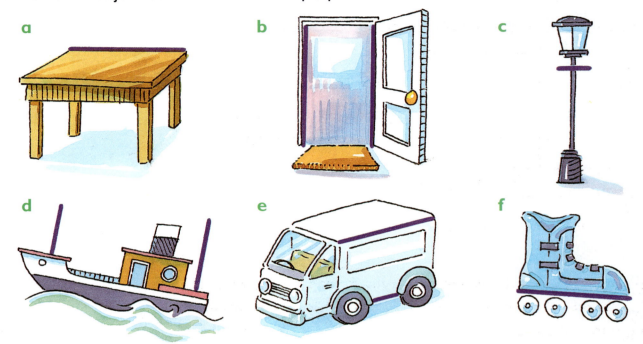

a b c
d e f

2 Copy these shapes on to dot lattice square paper.
   Use pencils or felt tip pens and colour the:
   • horizontal lines, blue
   • vertical lines, green
   • diagonal lines, orange.

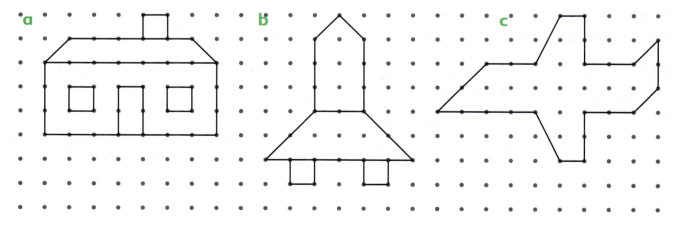

a b c

Sp 4, 5

Practice

You need: squared paper, blue, green and orange pencils or felt tip pens

1 In this spiral, some lines are horizontal and some are vertical.

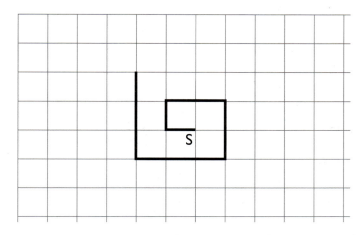

h means horizontal
v means vertical

   a Copy and continue the spiral on squared paper as far as you can go.
   b Colour the horizontal lines, blue and the vertical lines, green.
   c Copy and complete:
      1 h, 1 v, 2 h, 2 v, 3 h … and so on.

2 Draw and colour this spiral on squared paper.
   10 h, 9 v, 8 h, 7 v, 6 h, 5 v, 4 h, 3 v, 2 h, 1 v.

3 a Use a set square to draw this diagram in your exercise book.

   b Use you ruler to mark points 1 cm apart. Number the points 1 to 8.

   c Rule straight lines (diagonals) to join together a horizontal and a vertical point with the same number.

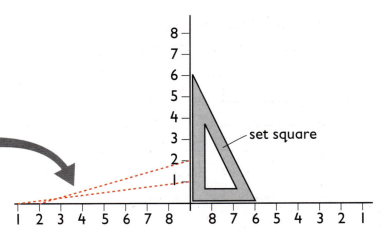

• Describe and visualise 2D shapes

Circles

Refresher

1 Fold a paper circle in half. Then fold it in half again. Mark and label the centre.

2 Draw and label a diameter and a radius. Stick the circle in your exercise book.

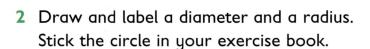

Practice

1. Measure the radius and diameter of these circles to the nearest half centimetre. Copy and complete this table.

circle	a	b	c	d	e	f
diameter						
radius						

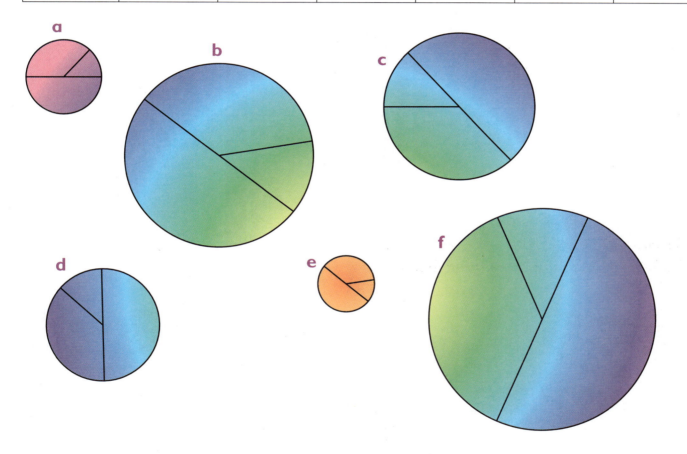

2. The diameter is always twice the length of the radius.

a. Draw 5 different circles. Measure each diameter and radius to check.

b. Copy and complete this sentence:
The radius is always …

- Use the eight compass directions N, S, E, W, NE, NW, SE, SW

Compass points

Refresher

Tom made this map of the places he visited in Austin, Texas.

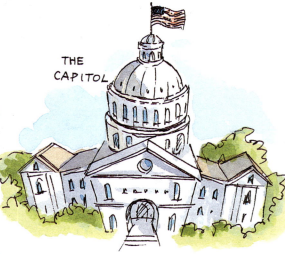

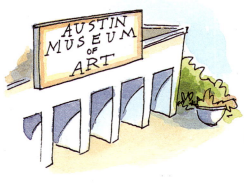

1 What is:

   a West of the State Capitol?   b North of the Governor's Mansion?

   c East of the Driskill Hotel?   d South of Ninfa's Mexican Food?

2 You are at the State Capitol. Which building is:

   a to the south-west   b to the north-east?   c to the north-west?

Practice

1 In which direction is the transport travelling?

Look at the map on page 26.
Imagine you are at the top of the State Capitol Building.

2 Face the Longhorns Football Stadium. Turn clockwise through 90° then 45°.

   a In which direction do you now face?   b Which building do you see?

3 Face Austin Airport. Turn anti-clockwise to face Allen's Boots Store. How many degrees do you turn through?

4 a Name the buildings you see as you turn clockwise from S to NW.

   b Through how many degrees do you turn?

5 You are facing Bark 'n' Purr.

   a In which direction are you facing?   b Which building lies in the opposite direction?

Routes and directions

Sp 5, 3

● Use the eight compass directions N, S, E, W, NE, NW, SE, SW

Refresher

1 a Copy this diagram and compass rose on squared paper.

   b Draw a NW route from the point (6, 0).

   c Write the co-ordinates of the points which your route passes through.

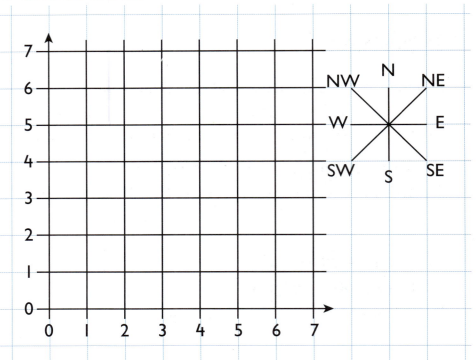

Practice

1 You need squared paper. Copy the diagram above.
   a Travel along the grid lines to all the points with a total distance of 6 units from the origin.

   b Write the co-ordinates of the points you land on.

2 A grid has been drawn on this plan of the baseball park to help you.
   a These fielders throw the ball to the pitcher.
      Write the direction of throw
      from — the catcher
      — fielder A
      — fielder B
      — fielder C
      — fielder D

   b In which direction does the ball travel
      — from 2nd base to 1st base?
      — from 2nd base to 3rd base?

   c Player B throws the ball NW. Which fielder will catch it? What if he throws SW? Who will catch the ball?

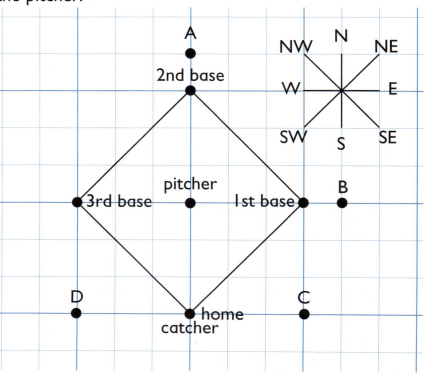

28

- Draw, measure and order a set of angles less than 180°

Sp 5, 4

Measuring angles

Refresher

The Zuni Indians, one of the Pueblo Indian tribes, live in the American state of New Mexico. They use the rain bird motif to decorate their pottery.
A rain bird has a hook-like head, a triangular body, two legs and three feathers.

1 Use your set squares to measure the size of each angle.
  Record the size of the angle at the **head**, **tail** and **body**.

head angle = 30°
tail angle = 60°
body angle = 90°

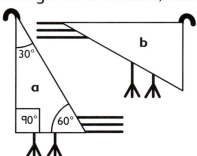

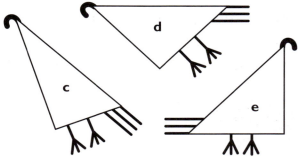

2 Use your set squares to design your own rain bird. Draw it in your exercise book.
  Measure and mark the size of each angle.

Practice

1 Copy and complete these sentences. Write > or < in the blank space.

a 60° ☐ 45°   b 45° ☐ 30°   c 45° ☐ 90°
d 90° ☐ 60°   e 45° + 30° ☐ 90°   f 60° + 45° ☐ 90°

2 Use a ruler and a set square to draw a triangle with:

a 2 angles of 45°

b 2 angles of 60°

c 1 angle of 45°, 1 angle of 60°

d 1 angle of 60°, 1 angle of 30°

e 1 angle of 30°, 1 angle of 45°

3 Using your set squares, measure and record the size of the third angle for each triangle in question 2.

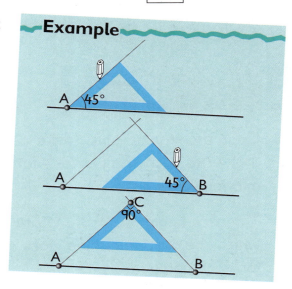

Example

- Estimate/check times using seconds, minutes, hours

Sp 5, 5

Race times

Refresher

1. Look at the results board.
   To qualify for the finals, each swimmer must finish the race in under one minute.

   a Write the name and the number of seconds for each finalist.

   b Write the names and times in minutes and seconds of the non-qualifiers.

Swimming results

Name	Seconds
Kevin	63
Mandy	57
Jacqui	53
Dougie	71
Imran	48
Lynn	66

Practice

Cross country results

Name	Minutes
Asrif	110
Brian	132
Chris	103
Darren	116
Emma	124
Frank	115
Greg	109
Hannah	121

1. a Who won the cross-country race?
   b Who came second?
   c How much faster was Greg than Emma?

Example
Ashrif 110 minutes = 1 hour 50 minutes

2. Copy the results table. Make a third column and write each competitor's time in hours and minutes.

3. The race began at 10:30. Write the time which the digital finishing clock showed for each competitor.

Example
Ashrif 12:20

- Visualise 3D shapes from 2D drawings and identify simple nets of solid shapes

Sp 6, 1

Working with 3D shapes

Refresher

1 Build these solid shapes with cubes.

a 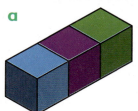   b    c 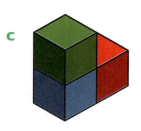   d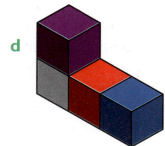

2 Take 4 cubes. Build a solid shape. Draw your shape on dot paper.

Practice

Example

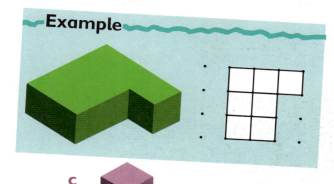

1 a Work out the least number of cubes you will need to build each shape.
   b Check by building each shape.
   c Draw your shape on dot paper.
   d Write down the number of cubes needed.

a    b 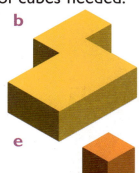   c

d    e 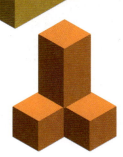   f

2 Predict which net cannot fold up to make a closed cube. Check by making the net with plastic interlocking squares. Remake the net so that it will work and record it on dot paper.

a   b   c   d

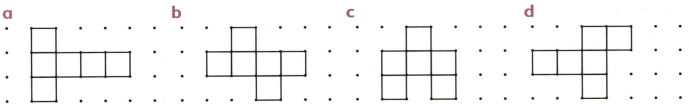

31

- Make shapes: for example construct polygons by paper folding or using pinboard and discuss properties

Sp 6, 2

Folding and cutting

Refresher

You need: A6 size rectangles of paper, scissors, glue
For each shape, start with a fresh sheet of A6 paper.
Fold your paper in half each time.

Example

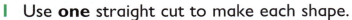

1. Use **one** straight cut to make each shape.

   a 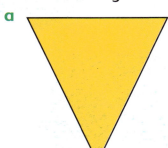   b    c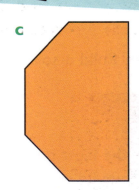

2. Find a way to make these shapes. Use two cuts around the fold line. Mark the line of symmetry and glue the shape into your exercise book.

   a 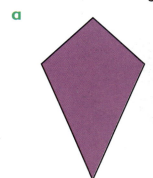   b    c

   d 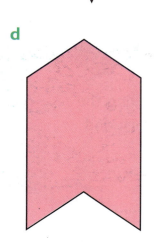   e 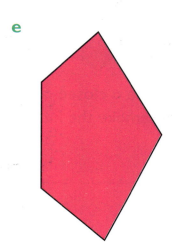   f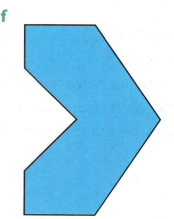

32

Practice

You need: A6 size rectangles of paper, scissors, glue

1. For each shape, start with a fresh sheet of A6 paper.
   Fold your paper in half, then in quarters.
   Try to make these shapes using one straight cut only.

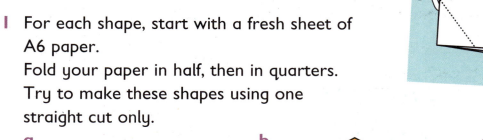

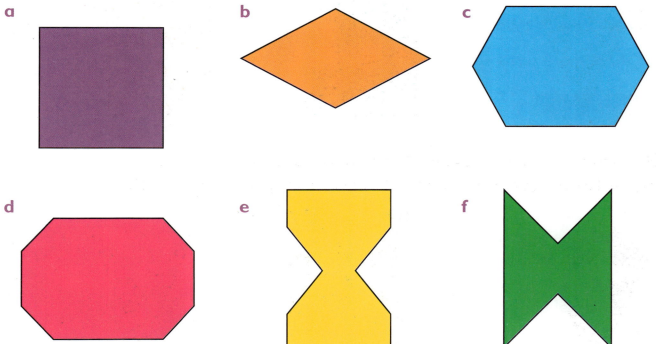

2. Fold your paper in half, then in thirds.
   a With one straight cut, make three different symmetrical shapes.
   b Mark the mirror lines and glue your shapes into your exercise book.

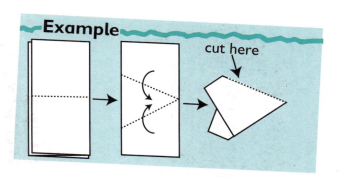

- Solve mathematical problems or puzzles, recognise and explain patterns and relationships, generalise and predict

Sp 6, 3

Investigating 3D shapes

Refresher

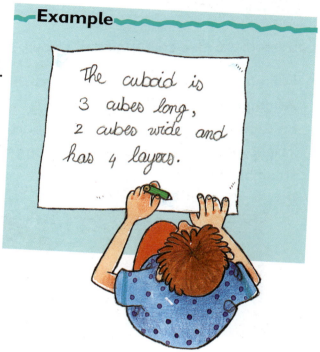

Example

The cuboid is 3 cubes long, 2 cubes wide and has 4 layers.

Work with a friend.
You need 24 cubes each and a small piece of paper.

1. Use all your cubes and build a cuboid.
2. Write a description of your cuboid.
3. Now swap papers.
4. Build each other's cuboids as described.
5. Have three more turns each.

Practice

Work with a partner.

1. You can arrange 36 cubes to make a 6 × 3 × 2 cuboid.
   How many different cuboids can you make with 36 cubes?

2. Make a table of your results.
   Try to work in a systematic way.
   Let's begin with 1 layer.

3.

What if we had 72 cubes? How many different cuboids could we make? Perhaps 12?

12 at least. I predict 16.

Which prediction is correct?
Investigate.

Counting forwards and backwards

Refresher

Copy and complete the number sequences.

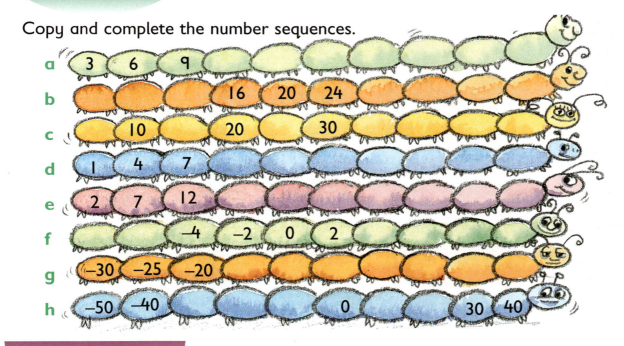

a 3 6 9
b   16 20 24
c 10   20   30
d 1 4 7
e 2 7 12
f   −4 −2 0 2
g −30 −25 −20
h −50 −40   0   30 40

Practice

In each building, find out which level the car park, photocopy room, lunch room and observation gallery are on. Use Reception or the ground floor as your starting point.

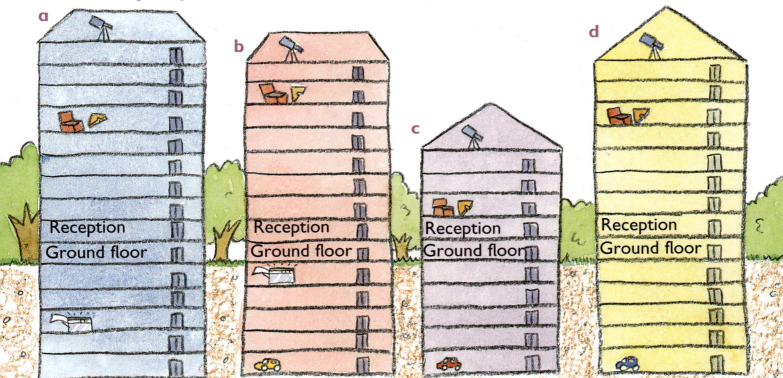

- Recognise and extend number sequences formed by counting from any number in steps of constant size

Sp 7, 2

Counting in 25s

Refresher

1 Complete each table by adding or subtracting 25 from the numbers shown.

a

	25	100	150	300	225	−75	0	−25
+25								

b

	25	100	150	0	75	−25	−75	200
−25								

Practice

Find your way to the treasure by following the correct sequence on the footsteps.

36

- Solve mathematical problems or puzzles, recognise and explain patterns and relationships

Sp 7, 3

Number investigations

Refresher

What different totals can you make?
Remember to do the calculation inside the brackets first!

a
- $(2 + 3 + 4) - 1 =$ ☐
- $(4 - 3) + 1 + 2 =$ ☐
- $(1 + 2 + 3) - 4 =$ ☐
- $(1 + 2 + 3) + 4 =$ ☐
- $(3 - 2) + 1 + 4 =$ ☐
- $(3 + 4 + 1) - 2 =$ ☐
- $(3 - 1) + 2 + 4 =$ ☐

b
- $(2 + 3) - (4 + 1) =$ ☐
- $(3 + 4) - (2 + 1) =$ ☐
- $(4 + 2) - (3 - 1) =$ ☐
- $(4 - 3) + (2 - 1) =$ ☐
- $(1 + 4) + (2 + 3) =$ ☐
- $(4 + 3) - (2 + 1) =$ ☐

Practice

Investigation

The children in Year 4 carried out an investigation.

Can you make 6 by using each of the digits 1, 2, 3 and 4 once and any of the operations + − × ÷?

Here are some of their results.

6
$(3 + 4 + 1) - 2 = 6$
$(4 - 2) + 1 + 3 = 6$
$(21 + 3) \div 4 = 6$
$(3 \times 4) \div (1 \times 2) = 6$

How many different ways of making the total 6 can you find?

Investigation

Using the same digits 1, 2, 3, 4 and any of the operations + − × ÷ the children made totals of the digits 1 to 6.

Here are their results.

$1 \rightarrow (3 \times 2) - 4 - 1$
$2 \rightarrow (3 + 2 + 1) - 4$
$3 \rightarrow (21 \div 3) - 4$
$4 \rightarrow (14 \div 2) - 3$
$5 \rightarrow (3 \times 4) \div 2 - 1$
$6 \rightarrow (12 \div 4) + 3$

Is it possible to make the numbers 7 up to 20? Record your results.

37

- Solve mathematical problems or puzzles, recognise and explain patterns and relationships

Sp 7, 4

Number combinations

Refresher

| 1 | 2 | 3 | 4 | 5 | 6 | 7 | 8 | 9 |

Each safe has a different combinations of 3 numbers to open it.
The combinations all add to make a total of 15.
Find a combination for each safe.

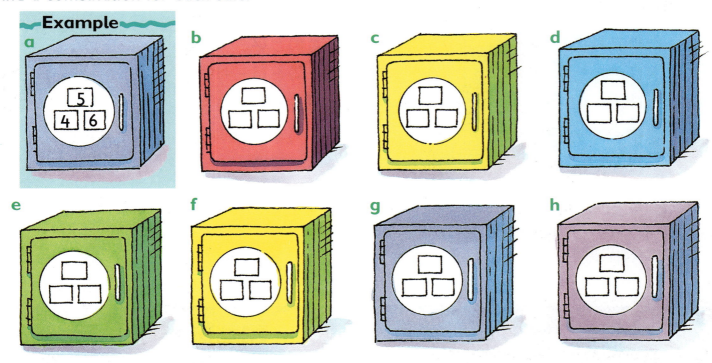

Practice

Use the numbers 1 to 9.
Arrange the numbers 1, 2, 3 …to 9 in the circles so that the sum of the numbers along each side of the pentagon matches the number in the centre.

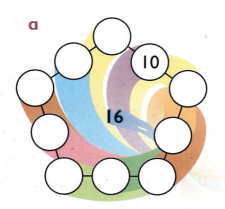
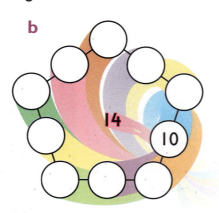
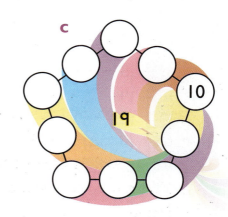

38

• Make and investigate a general statement about familiar numbers by finding examples that satisfy it   Sp 7, 5

Finding halfway between numbers

Refresher

1 a Write the number that is halfway between these sets of numbers.

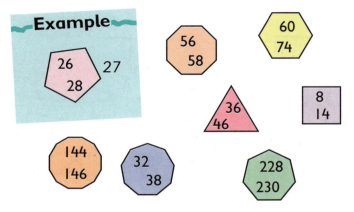

b Look carefully at each answer. What do you notice? Why has this happened?

2 a Write the number that is halfway between these sets of numbers.

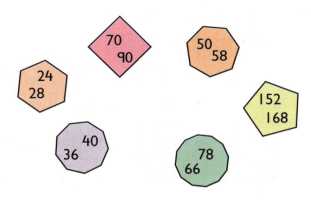

b Look carefully at each answer. What do you notice? Why has this happened?

Practice

Class 4 carried out two investigations. They drew number lines to help them. This is what they found.

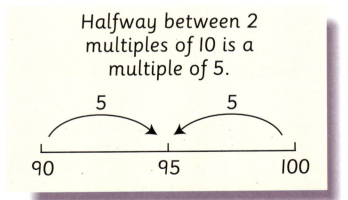

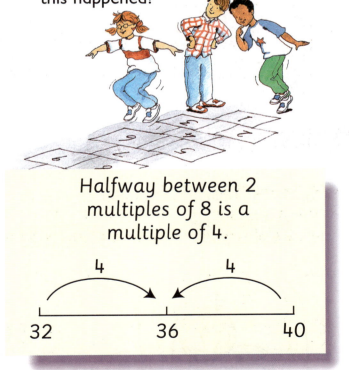

1 a Use multiples of 10 to find out if what they found is always true.
  b Write a statement to show what you found.

2 a Use multiples of 8 to find out if what they found is always true.
  b Write a statement to show what you found.

39

Revising multiplication and division facts

Refresher

For each jigsaw, write the related multiplication and division facts.

a) $5 \times 4 = 20$; $20 \div 5 = 4$; $4 \times 5 = 20$; $20 \div 4 = 5$

b) $30 \div 3 =$

c) $6 \times 5 =$

d) $4 \times 3 =$

e) $35 \div 5 =$

f) $4 \times 6 =$

Practice

1 Choose a marble from each jar to make up 15 multiplication number sentences.

2 Choose a marble from each jar to make up 15 division number sentences.

- Derive quickly doubles of multiples of 10 to 500 and the corresponding halves

Sp 8, 2

Doubles and halves

Refresher

1 Halve each of the numbers on the floats. Check your answer is correct by doubling.

Example
Half of 140 = 70
Double 70 = 140
or 140 ÷ 2 = 70
2 × 70 = 140

Practice

1 Double each number as you go down the slide. Write down each number.

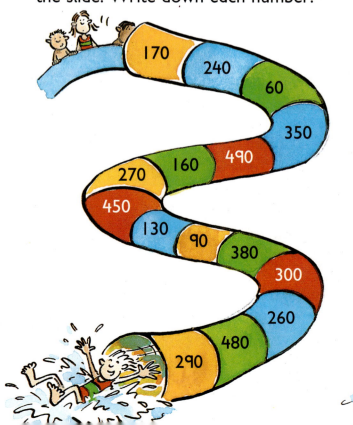

2 Halve each number as you go down the slide. Write down each number.

41

• Begin to know multiplication facts for the 6 times table

Sp 8, 3

Finding out about 6s

Refresher

The answers to the 6 times table are locked away in the treasure chest.
Search this page for the key facts and use them to help you work out the answers.

a
2 × 6 =
10 × 6 =
1 × 6 =
5 × 6 =

b
9 × 6 =
6 × 6 =
3 × 6 =
7 × 6 =

c
0 × 6 =
4 × 6 =
11 × 6 =
8 × 6 =

d
☐ × 6 = 24
☐ × 6 = 42
☐ × 6 = 60

e
6 × ☐ = 6
6 × ☐ = 54
6 × ☐ = 30

f
3 × ☐ = 18
☐ × 6 = 36
☐ × 6 = 12

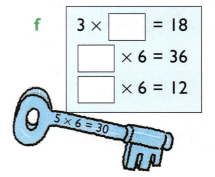

Practice

Use the strategy ☐ × 6 = ☐ × 4 add ☐ × 2 to find the answers.

Example
a   5 × 6
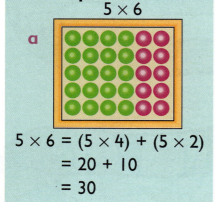

5 × 6 = (5 × 4) + (5 × 2)
= 20 + 10
= 30

e   4 × 6
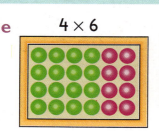

b   8 × 6

f   6 × 6
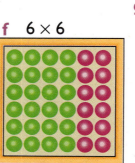

c   3 × 6
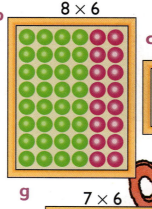

g   7 × 6
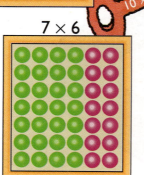

d   9 × 6
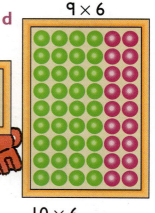

h   10 × 6
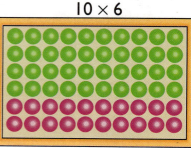

The 8 times table

Refresher

The answers to the 8 times table are locked away in the treasure chest.
Search this page for the key facts and use them to help you work out the answers.

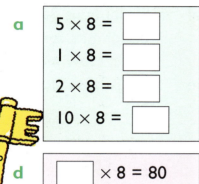
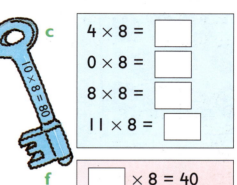

a
5 × 8 =
1 × 8 =
2 × 8 =
10 × 8 =

b
6 × 8 =
3 × 8 =
7 × 8 =
9 × 8 =

c
4 × 8 =
0 × 8 =
8 × 8 =
11 × 8 =

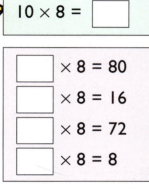

d
☐ × 8 = 80
☐ × 8 = 16
☐ × 8 = 72
☐ × 8 = 8

e
8 × ☐ = 0
8 × ☐ = 80
8 × ☐ = 64
8 × ☐ = 88

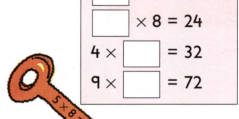

f
☐ × 8 = 40
☐ × 8 = 24
4 × ☐ = 32
9 × ☐ = 72

Practice

Complete each number fact for 4.
Double your answer to complete the multiplication fact for 8.

a 3 × 8 =

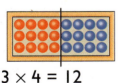

3 × 4 = 12
Double 12 = 24
3 × 8 = 24

b 8 × 8 =

c 6 × 8 =

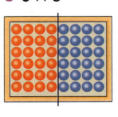

d 9 × 8 =

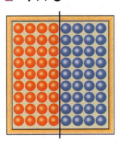

e 7 × 8 =

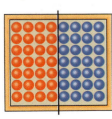

f 4 × 8 =

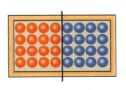

g 5 × 8 =

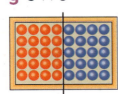

h 10 × 8 =

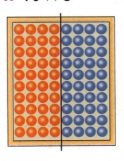

Solving word problems

Refresher

Read each problem. Decide whether you will use × or ÷.
Calculate the answer for each problem.

10 doughnuts per tray

a Mrs Smith buys 7 trays of doughnuts. How many doughnuts altogether?

b Julie puts 16 trays of doughnuts in the shop window. How many doughnuts are there altogether?

c Shelly buys 30 doughnuts for her class. How many trays does she buy?

d Sami orders 32 trays of doughnuts for her party. How many doughnuts in total?

e The baker has made a total of 250 doughnuts. How many trays does he need?

f 10 doughnuts cost £1. How much for 160 doughnuts?

Practice

Read each problem. Find the important information.
Write a division calculation for each problem.
Check to see that you have answered the question.

a Bags of flour cost £4 each. How many bags can be bought for £32? If bags of flour double in price, how many bags can be bought?

b Mr Michael bought 3 gateaux for his dinner party. He spent £24. How much did each gateau cost? How much for 6 gateaux?

c The bakery sold 4 birthday cakes on Monday. They made £28 altogether. How much for 1 cake? How much for 6 cakes?

d In one week, the bakery made £60 on chocolate biscuits. 10 packets were sold. How much per packet? How much money was made if only 6 packets were sold?

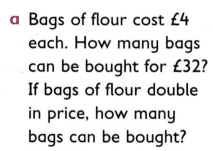

- Use closely related facts (e.g. to multiply by 9, multiply by 10 and adjust)

Sp 9, 1

Finding out about 9

Refresher

Multiply the number shown on each cash register by 10.
Write the new number.

a  b c  d  e

f  g  h  i  j

Practice

Example
$12 \times 9 = (12 \times 10) - 12$
$ = 120 - 12$
$ = 108$

1 Calculate the answers to these. Show your working.

a 7×9 b 13×9

c 16×9 d 9×9

e 14×9 f 15×9

g 6×9 h 18×9

i 27×9 j 22×9

To multiply by 9 I think: Multiply by 10 and adjust

2 Liz bought tiles to make a mosaic table.
Each tile cost £9.
Work out how much she paid for each of the colours she used.
Show your working.

TILES 'R' US
Yellow tiles
6 × £9 = ...
Red tiles
___ × £9 = ...
Blue tiles
___ × £9 = ...

- Use closely related facts (e.g. to multiply 11, multiply by 10 and adjust)

Sp 9, 2

Easy elevens

Refresher

1 Multiply the number on each balloon by 10. Write the new number.

Example
15 × 10 = 150

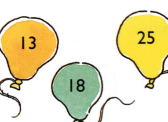

2 Multiply the number on each balloon by 1. Write the new number.

Example
7 × 1 = 7

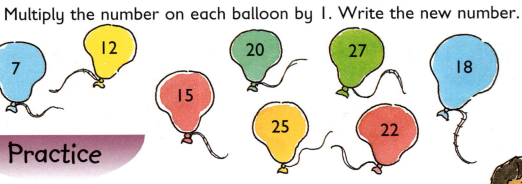

Practice

Throw 2 rings on to each game. Multiply the numbers landed on by 11 to get your score for each ring. Show your working.

Multiply by 10 first then add

a

14, 13, 16

Example
13 × 11 = (13 × 10) + 13
= 130 + 13
= 143

b
5, 12, 11

c
8, 17, 14

d

10, 20, 30

e
26, 18, 29

f
21, 19, 15

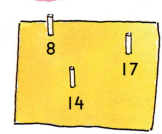

46

- Partition (e.g. $23 \times 4 = (20 \times 4) + (3 \times 4)$)

Sp 9, 3

Multiplying larger numbers

Refresher

Example
$26 \times 4 = (20 \times 4) + (6 \times 4)$

Partition each of these calculations.

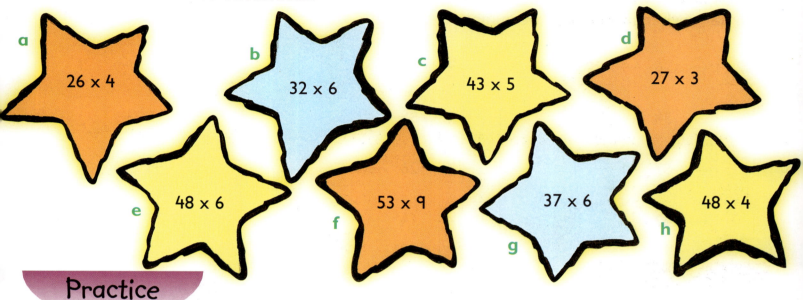

a 26 × 4
b 32 × 6
c 43 × 5
d 27 × 3
e 48 × 6
f 53 × 9
g 37 × 6
h 48 × 4

Practice

Approximate your answer first.
Then work out the answers by using the standard method of recording.

Example

$48 \times 3 \rightarrow (50 \times 3 = 150)$

```
           48
        ×   3
(40 × 3)  120
(8 × 3)    24
          ___
          144
```

a 46 × 3
b 32 × 6
c 29 × 5
d 16 × 4
e 23 × 5
f 48 × 3
g 54 × 5
h 25 × 5
i 34 × 4
j 43 × 6
k 18 × 3
l 27 × 5

Remember to keep the numbers in the correct columns
→ hundreds under hundreds
→ tens under tens
→ units under units

47

- Develop and refine written methods for TU x U – partitioning

Sp 9, 4

Recording multiplications

Refresher

Write the multiples of 10 each number is between.
Circle which multiple of 10 the number is closest to.

20	← 26 →	(30)		← 71 →			← 89 →	
[ ]	← 34 →	[ ]	[ ]	← 55 →	[ ]	[ ]	← 36 →	[ ]
[ ]	← 57 →	[ ]	[ ]	← 26 →	[ ]	[ ]	← 95 →	[ ]
[ ]	← 42 →	[ ]	[ ]	← 14 →	[ ]	[ ]	← 23 →	[ ]

Practice

Approximate your answer first. Then work out the answer by using the standard method of recording.

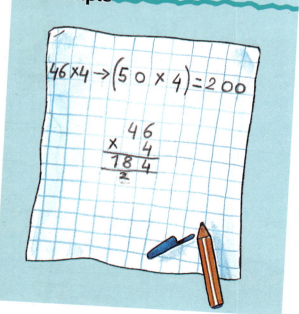

Example

a 27 × 5
b 43 × 6
c 25 × 5
d 48 × 3
e 16 × 4
f 32 × 6
g 18 × 3
h 34 × 4
i 54 × 5
j 46 × 3
k 29 × 5
l 23 × 5

Remember to keep the numbers in the correct columns
→ hundreds under hundreds
→ tens under tens
→ units under units

• Use × and ÷ to solve word problems involving numbers in "real life" and money …

Sp 9, 5

Solving word problems

Refresher

Read the story problems. Work out the answers in your head. Write the answer.

a John buys 7 climbing plants. How much does he spend?

b What is the total cost of 9 packs of garden tools?

c Mr Jones has £65. Does he have enough money to buy 6 climbing plants?

d How many terracotta pots can you buy with £90?

e Josie buys the last two garden hoses. How much does she spend?

Practice

Read the story problems. Choose an appropriate method of calculating your answer.

- mental
- mental with jottings
- pencil and paper

a John buys 2 garden manuals. How much does he spend?

b Mrs Clarke buys 4 climbing plants. Mr Clarke buys 6 terracotta pots. Who spends the most money?

c The garden shop has 37 rose bushes to sell. How much money will they make?

d Jim, the gardener, has enough money to buy 57 packets of seeds. How much money does he have?

e Joanna has £100. She buys 24 packets of seeds and 2 packets of tools. What else can she buy with her change?

- Identify two simple fractions with a total of 1

Sp 10, 1

Total fractions

Refresher

1 What fraction is one square?

a 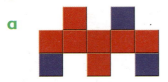   b   c   d

a tenth $\frac{1}{10}$

e    f    g    h

2 Write the fraction of red squares.
Write the fraction of blue squares.

Practice

1 Make a shape using up to 10 cubes in 2 colours.
Write the fraction of squares for each colour.
Make 5 shapes like this:

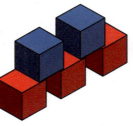

blue   red
$\frac{2}{5} + \frac{3}{5} = 1$

2 Make 5 more shapes using up to 10 cubes in 3 colours.

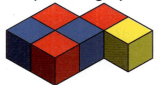

red   blue   yellow
$\frac{3}{6} + \frac{2}{6} + \frac{1}{6} = 1$

3 Copy and fill in the missing fractions.

a $\frac{3}{4} + \boxed{} = 1$ b $\frac{1}{6} + \boxed{} = 1$

c $\frac{2}{5} + \boxed{} = 1$ d $\boxed{} + \frac{3}{8} = 1$

e $\frac{4}{10} + \boxed{} = 1$ f $\boxed{} + \frac{2}{7} = 1$

g $\boxed{} + \frac{5}{9} = 1$ h $\frac{3}{10} + \frac{4}{10} + \boxed{} = 1$

i $\frac{1}{9} + \frac{2}{9} + \boxed{} = 1$ j $\frac{2}{7} + \boxed{} + \frac{2}{7} = 1$

Bottle top fractions

Refresher

Half the bottle tops are red. Write other fractions to show half.

a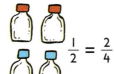

b

c

d

d

e

f

Practice

Write two fractions for the red bottle tops.

a

b

c

d

e

f

g

h

i

j

k

l

m

n

o

- Order simple fractions: for example, decide whether fractions such as $\frac{3}{8}$ or $\frac{7}{10}$ are greater or less than one half

Sp 10, 3

Fraction order

Refresher

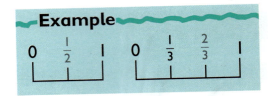

1 Copy the number lines. Fill in the missing fractions.

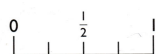

2 Circle the fractions that are greater than $\frac{1}{2}$.

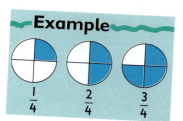

Practice

1 Copy the table.

less than $\frac{1}{2}$	equal to $\frac{1}{2}$	greater than $\frac{1}{2}$
$\frac{1}{4}$	$\frac{2}{4}$	$\frac{3}{4}$

Choose a circle and copy it. Colour its parts one by one.
Write the fractions coloured in the table.

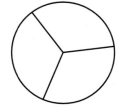 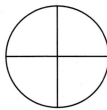   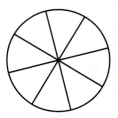 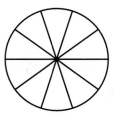

2 Write these fractions in order, smallest to largest.

a $\frac{4}{5}, \frac{2}{5}, \frac{1}{5}$

b $\frac{3}{8}, \frac{2}{8}, \frac{5}{8}$

c $\frac{9}{10}, \frac{5}{10}, \frac{6}{10}, \frac{3}{10}$

d $\frac{5}{6}, \frac{1}{6}, \frac{3}{6}$

e $\frac{3}{4}, 0, \frac{1}{4}, 1$

f $\frac{7}{8}, \frac{1}{8}, \frac{6}{8}, \frac{4}{8}$

• Understand decimal notation and place value for tenths and hundreds, and use it in context   Sp 10, 4

Daredevil decimals

Refresher

1 Write the fractions as decimals.

a 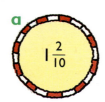 b 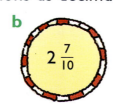 c 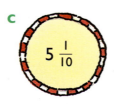 d 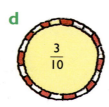 e 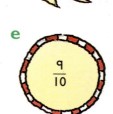 f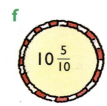

$1\frac{2}{10}$ $2\frac{7}{10}$ $5\frac{1}{10}$ $\frac{3}{10}$ $\frac{9}{10}$ $10\frac{5}{10}$

2 Write the decimals as fractions.

a	b	c	d	e	f
3·4	0·8	12·2	0·6	35·3	0·1

Practice

1 Copy the number line.

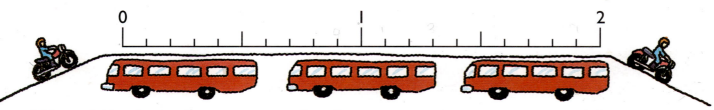

Write these decimals on your number line.

1·1   0·9   1·3   0·2   1·9   0·5

2 Copy the number line.

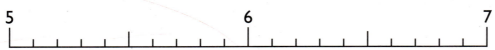

Write these decimals on your number line.

6·5   5·1   6·9   5·5   6·3   5·7

3 Write these weights in order, smallest to largest.

a 0·5kg 10·3kg 0·7kg   b 1·2kg 0·6kg 0·2kg   c 5·9kg 11·2kg 5·2kg
   1kg   0·1kg   2kg   1·6kg 1·1kg   7·1kg 9·3kg   7·4kg

53

- Understand decimal notation and place value for tenths and hundredths

Sp 10, 5

Decimal amounts

Refresher

Write the amounts using pounds and pence notation.

a   b   c   d

Practice

1 Write these prices in pence.

a £1·92   b £5·04   c £8·50   d £0·64   e £0·08

2 Write these prices in £.

a 461p   b 95p   c 230p   d 6p   e 403p

3 Write these prices in order, highest to lowest.

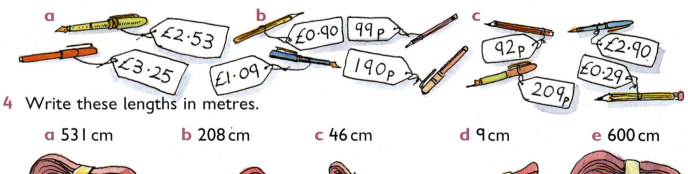

a £2·53   £3·25   £1·09
b £0·90   99p   190p
c 92p   £2·90   £0·29   209p

4 Write these lengths in metres.

a 531 cm   b 208 cm   c 46 cm   d 9 cm   e 600 cm

5 Write these lengths in order, shortest to longest.

2·47 m   0·47 m   4·72 m   2·74 m   7·24 m   0·27 m

Questionnaire bar charts

Refresher

Questionnaire

Which country would you like to go to for a holiday?

Tick one box.

Germany ☐   France ☐

Spain ☐   Italy ☐

The bar chart shows children's favourite country to go for a holiday.

a Copy the bar chart.

b 12 children chose Germany. Draw the bar.

c How many children chose Spain?

d Which is the most popular country?

e Which is the least popular country?

f How many more children chose France than Italy?

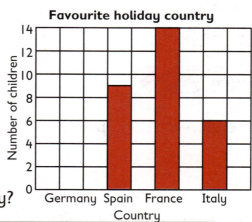

Practice

Questionnaire

Which after school club do you like best?

Tick one box only.

Sport ☐   Drama ☐

Chess ☐   Computing ☐

The frequency table shows children's favourite after school clubs.

Club	Number of children
Sport	11
Chess	7
Drama	8
Computing	9

a Copy these axes. Draw a bar chart.

b Which club is the most popular?

c Which club is the least popular?

d More children chose Sport than Chess. How many more?

e How many chose Chess or Drama?

f How many children answered the questionnaire?

g Which are the two favourite clubs?

- Solve a given problem by collecting quickly, organising, representing and interpreting data in tables

Dice bar charts

Refresher

Janice rolled a die lots of times. The bar chart shows her results.

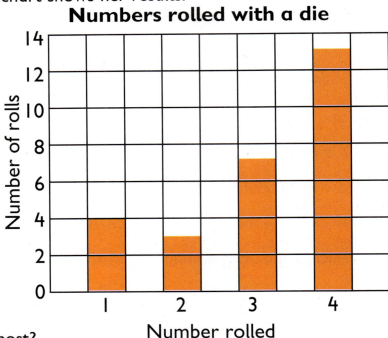

1 a How many times did she throw 1?

b Which number did she throw the most?

c Which number was thrown 7 times?

d Which number is least likely to be thrown?

e How many more 4s than 3s did she throw?

f How many times did she throw the die altogether?

2 Copy and complete Janice's tally chart.

Number rolled	Tally	Number of die rolls
1		
2		
3		
4		

Sp 11, 2

Practice

Work in pairs.
You will need: a blank die numbered 1, 2, 2, 2, 3, 4

1. Draw a tally chart.
   One player throws the die. The other makes a tally mark.

2. Count the tally marks.
   Write the frequencies in your tally chart.

3. Copy and complete the bar chart to show your results.

Number rolled	Tally	Frequency
1	||	
2	⋕ |||	
3	⋕	
4	||	

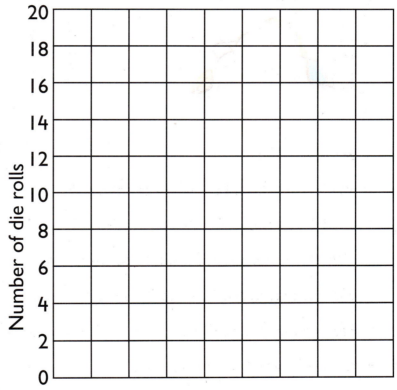

Number rolled with die

4   a How many twos did you throw?   b Which number was thrown the most?

    c Which number was thrown the least?   d How many times were 3 or 4 thrown?

5   Look at Janice's bar chart on page 56.

    a Who threw the most 3s, you or Janice?   b How many times did you throw your die?

    c Who threw the most times, you or Janice?   d Do you think your die is different from Janice's? How is it different?

• Solve a problem by collecting quickly, organising, representing and interpreting data in tables ...

Sweet shop bar charts

Refresher

The bar chart shows the sweets in a bag.

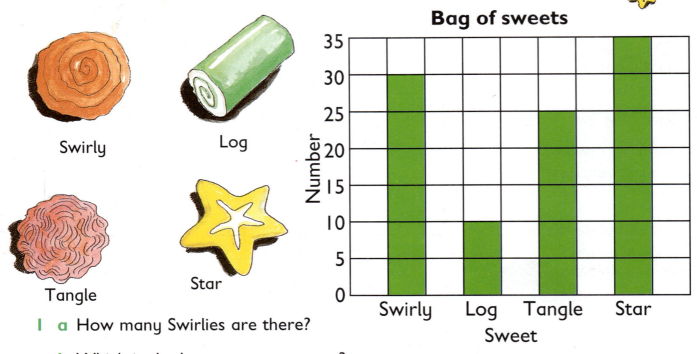

1 a How many Swirlies are there?

   b Which is the least common sweet?

   c There are 10 of one type of sweet. Which sweet?

   d Lee took a sweet from the bag without looking. Which sweet is it most likely to be?

   e Lee ate 10 Tangle sweets. How many does he have left?

   f How many sweets are in a bag?

2 Copy and complete the tally chart.

Sweet	Tally	Frequency
Swirly		

Sp 11, 3

Practice

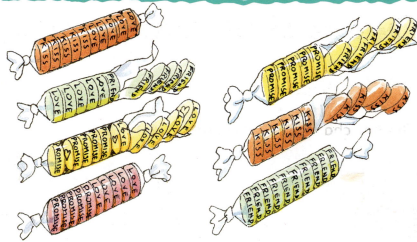

1 Copy and complete the tally chart.

Sweet	Tally	Frequency

2 Copy and complete the bar chart.

Sweet words

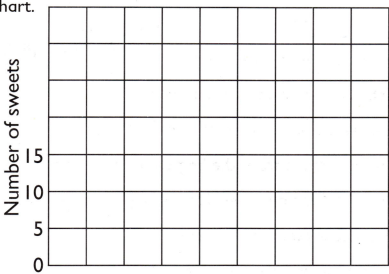

3 a Which sweet does the shop have most to sell?

  b How many more Love than Kiss sweets are there?

  c How many sweets are not Love sweets?

  d The shop sells 10 Friend and 5 Love sweets. Which sweet is there most of now?

  e How many sweets are Kiss or Friend?

  f Beverley bought 10 Kiss and 5 Love sweets. How many sweets are left in the shop?

59

Dog race bar chart

60

Refresher

Work in pairs.
You will need:
a 1–6 die, a counter

1 Copy this score table.

2 Put the counter on START.
Throw the die and move that number of spaces.
Record the score in the table. When you reach Finish,
calculate the total score for each dog.

Dog	Score	Total
Dawg		
Pooch		
Smooch		
Spot		

Practice

1 Copy and complete the bar chart for your scores.

2 a Which dog has the highest score?

   b What is the lowest score?

   c What is the total score for Pooch and Smooch?

   d Find the greatest difference between two scores.

   e How many times did you land on Smooch?

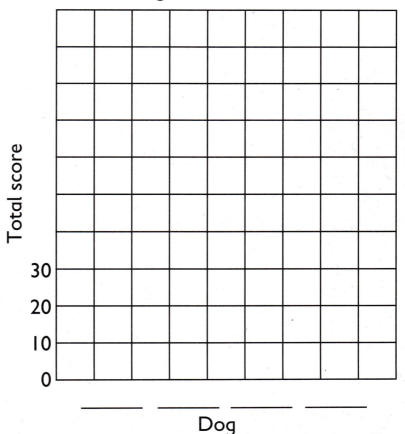

Dog race results

• Solve a problem by collecting quickly, organising, representing and interpreting data in tables ...

Money box bar charts

Refresher

1 Count the money belonging to each child.

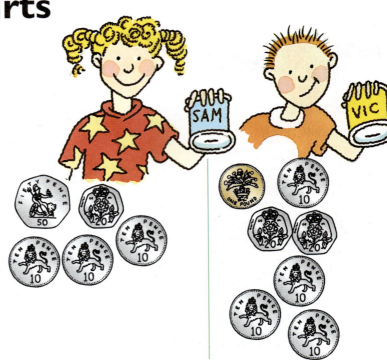

2 Write the totals in pence, in this table.

Name	Amount saved
Jan	
Ajit	
Sam	
Vic	

3 Copy and complete the bar chart.

4 a Which child saved the most?

   b Who saved £1?

   c Jan saved more than Ajit. How much more?

   d What does the shortest bar show?

   e How much money did Sam and Vic save together?

   f Ajit's bar grew to the top of the bar chart. How much more did he save?

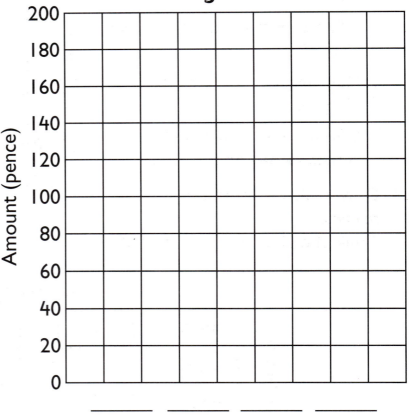

Sp 11, 5

Practice

1 Draw a bar chart to show the savings.

2 a Which money box has the most money?

   b What does the tallest bar of your chart show?

   c How much money is there altogether?

   d Which coins could be in the sweets money box?

3 Draw a pictogram to show the savings.
   Think of a picture to represent 20p.

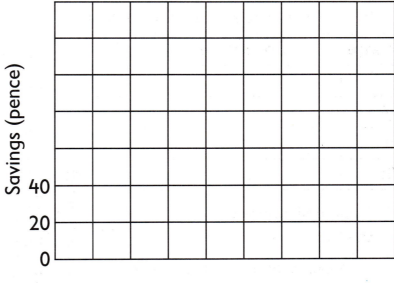

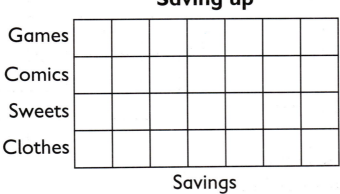

63